50

fantastic things to do with
Babies

SALLY AND PHILL FEATHERSTONE

Featherstone

Contents

Published 2010 by A&C Black Publishers Limited
36 Soho Square, London, W1D 3QY
www.acblack.com

ISBN 978-1-4081-2323-2

Written by Sally Featherstone and Phill Featherstone
Design by Bob Vickers
Photographs © Shutterstock 2010

Printed in Great Britain by Latimer Trend & Company Limited

A CIP record for this publication is available from the British Library.

This book is produced using paper that is made from wood grown in managed, sustainable forests. It is natural, renewable and recyclable. The logging and manufacturing processes conform to the environmental regulations of the country of origin.

To see our full range of titles
Visit www.acblack.com/featherstone

Introduction

There's plenty of research to show that babies and children who enjoy a stimulating home environment learn better and more quickly. So what parents and carers do to lay the groundwork for learning early on is an investment that pays back throughout their child's life.

This book has been specially written for parents to use with their babies at home. However, it can also be used by carers and workers in nurseries and child care settings. It contains 50 simple activities that can be done easily with very little equipment, often in odd moments of time. It's not a course to work through. All the ideas here are suitable for babies from soon after birth to around 20 months, and in many cases beyond. Some are more suited to younger babies and some to older. It's obvious which these are. Choose what you and your baby enjoy. When you find an activity you like, do it again, and again, and again. Babies love repetition and benefit from it.

Finally, please remember that one of the main aims of this book is fun. There are few things as delightful or rewarding as being alongside young children as they explore, enquire, experiment and learn. Join them in their enthusiasm for learning, and enjoy being with them!

There are four books in the 50 Fantastic Things series:

50 Fantastic Things to Do With Babies (suitable for use from soon after birth to 20 months)

50 Fantastic Things to Do With Toddlers (suitable for use from 16–36 months)

50 Fantastic Things to Do With Pre-Schoolers (suitable for use from 30–50 months)

50 Fantastic Things to Do With Four and Five Year Olds (suitable for use from 40–60+ months)

The age groupings above are approximate and are only suggestions. Children develop at different speeds. They also grow in spurts, with some periods of rapid development alternating with other times when they don't seem to change as quickly. So don't worry if your baby doesn't seem ready for a particular activity. Try another instead and return to it later. On the other hand, if your baby gets on well and quickly, try some of the ideas in the 'Another idea' and 'Ready for more?' sections.

A NOTE ON SAFETY

Care must be taken at all times when dealing with babies and young children. Common sense will be your main guide, but here are a few ideas to help you have fun safely.

Babies and young children naturally explore things by bringing them to their mouths. This is fine, but always check that toys and other objects you use are clean.

Although rare, swallowing objects or choking on them are hazards. Some children are more susceptible than others. If you are concerned about choking, buy a choke measure from a high street baby shop.

Baby's lungs are delicate. They need clean air. *Never* smoke near your baby, and don't allow anyone else to do so.

Children are naturally inquisitive and you will want to encourage this. However, secure and happy children are often unaware of danger. Your baby needs you to watch out for them. Make sure you are always there. You can't watch your baby all the time, but don't leave him/her alone and unsupervised for more than a few minutes at a time. Even when they are asleep check on them regularly.

The objects and toys we suggest here have been chosen for their safety. Nevertheless, most things can be dangerous if they go wrong or are not used properly:

- Mobiles and toys tied to baby gyms are great to encourage looking and reaching, but check that they are fastened securely.

- Ribbons and string are fascinating to babies but can be a choking hazard. They can also become wrapped round arms, legs and necks.

- Babies are natural explorers. They need clean floors. Store outdoor shoes away from areas where your baby will be lying and crawling.

- If your baby is just learning to balance, either sitting or standing, make sure they have a soft landing. Put a pillow behind babies who are starting to sit. If your baby is starting to crawl or walk, look out for trip hazards.

- Take care with furniture. Make sure your baby is fastened securely into his/her high chair. Pad sharp edges of tables and other furniture.

What is your baby learning?

Contact with you and watching your face is important in learning to talk. As you do this activity more, your baby will probably start to respond by smiling, wriggling and babbling. Don't worry if this takes time, or if sometimes they're just not in the mood.

Let's look
making contact

What you need:

• *No special equipment for this activity.*

Ready for more?

Make movements with your lips and mouth. See if your baby copies you.

Do the same activity facing a mirror so you can both see both of you.

WHAT TO DO:

1. Sit holding your baby in your lap, facing you. Rest your arms on a cushion if that helps.

2. Make sure your face is near enough for your baby to see you clearly (but not too close).

3. Talk or sing softly to your baby. Watch your baby's face all the time.

DID YOU KNOW? Young babies focus best on faces and objects held at between 20 and 25cm (8–10 inches) away.

4. As you talk, sometimes open your mouth wide or stick out your tongue. Watch to see if your baby copies your expression.

5. Move your head slowly from side to side and watch how your baby follows your face with their eyes.

6. Keep talking, singing and smiling.

Another idea: Put on a hat or a pair of glasses and try the same activity again.

First faces
fun with face patterns

What you need:

- a small paper plate or circle of white card
- a black marker or crayon (a lipstick will do instead)
- a chopstick, pencil or wooden spoon for a handle
- some sticky tape

WHAT TO DO:

1. Draw a face on a paper plate or a circle of card. Keep it very simple – eyes and mouth are all that's needed.

2. Glue or tape the 'face' on to a stick.

3. Put your baby in a baby chair or prop them up with a pillow.

4. Hold the face puppet close to the baby's face (20–25cm away).

5. Talk to your baby while you move the face slowly from side to side. Only move the face a few centimetres each way. Watch your baby's eyes and slow down or stop if they stop following.

6. If the baby reaches out to touch the face help by gently guiding their hand.

Another idea: Draw some more faces with different expressions. Keep them simple.

Ready for more?

Make another 'face puppet'. Glue this one upside down on the stick. Use both puppets and see which face your baby likes best.

Glue a plastic toy (a bath duck, plastic car, small doll) on a stick. Play with that in the same way and see how your baby responds.

HELPFUL HINTS

Don't move the puppet face too quickly. Move it gradually closer and further away and watch carefully to find where your baby can see it best.

Keep these sessions short or your baby may become tired.

What is your baby learning?

Playing this game will help your baby to recognise faces and movement, and will help them to focus their eyes. Watch for them following your movements and responding to the paper plate face by making sounds, smiling or staring.

HELPFUL HINTS
Watch for signs of agitation and stop at once if your baby seems not to be enjoying the activity.
Never leave small babies alone with pieces of fabric – they could become entangled.

What is your baby learning?

Playing this game will help your baby learn to copy and imitate. Look for them responding by making sounds, smiling and waving their limbs.

Hide and find

peep-bo, there you are!

What you need:
- *a piece of fabric, thin enough to see through (a net curtain, a piece of voile, a chiffon scarf)*

WHAT TO DO:

1. Sit your baby in your lap facing you, or opposite you in a baby chair.

2. Smile and talk to your baby. Tell them about the game.

3. Hold the fabric up between you so your face is hidden. Keep talking or singing.

4. Slowly lower the fabric so you can see each other, saying, 'There you are!'

5. Don't go too fast at first – your baby will need time to understand the concept.

6. Now put the fabric right over your head and slowly pull it off, talking all the time.

Another idea: Play the same game again, using thicker fabric, such as a towel or tea towel.

Ready for more?

Place the fabric gently over your baby's head and slowly pull it off. Talk all the time. **Some babies don't like their faces covered. Stop at once if they become agitated.**

As your baby gets used to the game use fabrics that are harder to see through.

DID YOU KNOW?

The shape of the human face is the first thing a baby learns to recognise.

Mirror, mirror
mirrors and shiny objects

What you need:
- *a shallow basket or tray*
- *a baby's safety mirror*
- *as many shiny objects as you can find (a metal serving spoon, a pan lid, shiny toys)*

Ready for more?

Line a shoebox with shiny paper. Fill it with a selection of different, brightly coloured objects. Explore the contents with your baby.

Stick some black tape to a mirror to make stripes or patterns on the surface.

WHAT TO DO:

1. Clear a space and remove other distractions. Sit your baby in a baby chair or prop them up with a cushion.

2. Place all the shiny objects and the mirror in the basket.

3. Sit opposite your baby and hold the mirror where they can look into it. Tap the mirror to encourage them to reach for it.

4. Sing or chant, 'Look (baby's name), who can I see? I can see you!' Tap the reflection and then gently stroke your baby's face.

5. Offer your baby other shiny things to explore. Look for reflections and sing again.

6. Allow plenty of time for exploring and repetition.

Another idea: Get hold of some shiny and reflective paper and shiny fabric. Explore it together.

DID YOU **KNOW?**

Babies find it easiest to see objects and patterns that have a strong contrast e.g. black on white.

What is your baby learning?

Playing this game will help your baby learn to copy and imitate. Look for them responding by making sounds, smiling and waving their limbs.

HELPFUL HINTS

Your baby might need you to take their hands and guide them gently to the objects.

Allow your baby plenty of time to lift his or her head to look and focus.

Rock star
rocking and feeling safe

What you need:
- *a blanket or a square of fleece*

WHAT TO DO:

1. Sit on the floor with your knees bent and slightly apart and your feet firmly on the floor. Hold your baby gently facing you, wrapped snugly in a blanket, so that you can easily look into each other's faces.

2. Sing this song to your baby. The tune to Frère Jaques fits, but if you like you can choose or make up your own. Keep it slow and steady.

> *Rock together, rock together,*
> *Here we go, to and fro.*
> *Rocking very gently, rocking very gently*
> *To and fro, here we go.*

3. As you sing the rhyme, rock gently together to the song. Start and finish gently.

4. Smile and hold the baby's gaze as you sing and rock.

Another idea: Sing the song while you rock your baby in her or his pushchair.

Ready for more?

Rock a teddy bear or soft toy from side to side as you sing the rhyme.

If your baby is older, sit him or her in a large box or plastic crate. Rock it gently from side to side as you sing the song.

DID YOU KNOW?

Babies are sensitive to rhythm from their earliest days.

HELPFUL HINTS

If your baby needs extra reassurance play the game standing up, holding him or her closely, snuggled in to your shoulder.

You can also rock with your baby by simply holding their hands.

What is your baby learning?

This game will lead to the development of balance and to expressing feelings.

Watch your baby carefully to see if he or she is looking, concentrating, showing pleasure and later swaying.

See here
copying facial expressions

What you need:
- *a floppy hat*
- *a pair of plastic sunglasses*

WHAT TO DO:

1. Make sure your baby is sitting comfortably and well supported. Sit opposite your baby so that your faces are at a similar level.

2. Give your baby the floppy hat to feel. Hold out your hand and help your baby to pass you the hat.

3. Pop the hat on your head and sing

    Where is my hat? Where is my hat?

    to the tune of 'Frère Jacques'. When baby is looking at you, tip the hat suddenly off your head, and say, 'Gone!'

4. Wait to see if your baby looks at or reaches for the hat. Play the game again.

5. Try the same game with the sunglasses.

Another idea: Look out for tinsel wigs and novelty sunglasses from fairs and novelty shops. These are great for encouraging looking.

DID YOU KNOW?
Babies find it easiest to see the colours black and yellow.

Ready for more?

Help your baby to put the hat on their head. Sing the song and then gently tip it off into their lap.

Put the hat on a teddy or doll and sing the song, tipping off the hat at the end.

What is your baby learning?

This game helps to develop attention and encourages first words.

HELPFUL HINTS

Your baby may be anxious when your appearance changes. Go slowly, and keep peeping out from under the hat so that they can see it's still you.

Help your baby to use two hands together.

Reach out
reaching and touching

What you need:
- a blanket

Ready for more?

Put a light scarf over your head and let baby pull it off.

Stand in front of a mirror and help your baby to reach out for the reflection.

WHAT TO DO:

1. Hold your baby securely so they can see your face. Make sure you have his or her attention.

2. Open your mouth wide and encourage baby to reach out and touch your face. Praise any movement he or she makes towards you with their hands or arms.

3. Now lie your baby on his or her back, on a blanket on the floor.

4. Lean over baby until your face is within reach. Talk to them and encourage them to reach up and touch your face. Remember to give praise and smiles for every effort at reaching, touching, holding.

Another idea: Hang a small object round your neck and lean over so baby can reach up for it.

What is your baby learning?

This game will help your baby learn to reach out and take turns. Watch your baby to see if she or he is looking, holding, grasping and making sounds.

DID YOU
KNOW?
*Young babies can't
see very far or judge
distances, so be ready
to help in the early
stages.*

Take this
holding and letting go

What you need:

- *a few everyday objects, small and light enough for baby to hold; e.g. a small whisk, a little wooden or baby spoon, a plastic lid, a small plastic toy*

WHAT TO DO:

1. Make sure your baby is sitting comfortably and well supported. Sit opposite your baby so that your faces are at a similar level.

2. Hold out one of the objects. Talk to baby and encourage them to take the object. Hold it close enough for them to be able touch it, but far enough away so they have to reach out.

3. Let your baby play with the object, talking to them about it as they do. Smile and praise them for holding it.

4. Offer another object and praise your baby if they take it.

5. Allow time to play with the objects and experiment.

Another idea: Use some crinkly paper or textured fabric instead of an object.

Ready for more?

Make a treasure basket for your baby to play with. Fill it with interesting objects to explore and hold.

Make a 'pat mat' from a small zip-lock bag filled with cotton wool, crinkly paper or even paint.

What is your baby learning?

This game helps your baby to grow and develop the muscles they need to control their hands and arms (important later when they learn to write).

HELPFUL HINTS

Make sure the objects are light enough for your baby to grip and wave about.

Don't rush things. Sit with your baby as they explore the objects, encouraging them and praising effort.

Shake it all about!
shaking and rattling

What you need:

- *some things that rattle – e.g. wrist rattles, tins containing beads or pasta, baby rattles, bells, boxes, purses with coins, snack tubes with small pebbles, zip-lock bags with beads*

WHAT TO DO:

1. Collect together a few rattling objects. Make sure they are light enough for your baby to hold and shake.

2. Sit opposite your baby and pick up one of the rattlers. Shake it to attract their attention.

3. Shake the rattle rhythmically, saying 'Look, look, look. Shake, shake, shake'.

4. Offer the rattle and wait for your baby to respond to it. Give it a little shake to tempt them.

5. Try having a rattle each and sharing the shaking.

Another idea: Play with bells, maracas and other simple musical instruments.

Ready for more?

Allow plenty of time for listening and for your baby to respond. Give lots of smiles and praise their efforts.

Try rattling under a blanket or cloth and see if they can pull the blanket off to get the rattle.

What is your baby learning?

In this game your baby is responding to sound and rhythm. Interacting with you will help them learn to relate to people. Look for grasping, smiling, shaking and signs of listening.

DID YOU KNOW?

There's a strong link between a child's ability to keep a steady beat and success at school.

Snuggle up
feeling close, feeling good

DID YOU KNOW?

Babies like to be held tight, it makes them feel secure. But don't squeeze too hard!

What you need:

- a soft blanket
- one of your baby's comfort toys
- soothing music and a soft lamp

WHAT TO DO:

1. Sit with your baby on your lap, so that they can easily see your face. Remember that she or he will focus best at 20–25cm.

2. Place the lamp where your baby can see it, at eye level but not so that it will dazzle them.

3. Give your baby their comfort toy and help them to hold it in their arms. Gently spread the blanket over both of you.

4. Sing hello to your baby, stroking their cheek softly as you sing their name.

5. Switch on the lamp and the music. Tap the light gently to draw attention to it, and sing:

   'Hello (baby's name), hello (baby's name), let's look, let's look, let's look.'

Ready for more?

Play a simple clapping game and sing 'Good morning baby, good morning (baby's name), good morning baby, let's say hello'.

Another idea: Sit with baby on your knee, facing away from you, holding their comfort toy in front of them. Make the comfort toy dance and then bring it to the baby for a hug.

What is your baby learning?

This activity helps to develop a sense of security and belonging, important for self-esteem.

HELPFUL HINTS

Make sure your baby's head is well supported.
Some babies can't yet regulate their body temperature. Make sure they don't get too hot under the blanket.

What is your baby learning?

This activity helps to develop your baby's concentration and will reinforce their bond with you. Watch for them showing pleasure and responding to your attention.

Say it with music
rocking and dancing a greeting

What you need:

- *two wrist toys or hair scrunchies*

WHAT TO DO:

1. Slip a wrist toy or hair scrunchie over your baby's wrist and put one on your own wrist.

2. Stand up, holding your baby facing you and close to your body.

3. Sway gently and rhythmically, dancing with and smiling at your baby. Hold your baby's hand and gently shake it, singing

    Good to see you, thanks for coming, hello (baby's name),
    Good to see you, thanks for coming, hello (baby's name).

The song should be lively and bouncy, but be careful you don't shake your baby up and down too much.

Another idea: Change your song. Put on some bouncy music and sing along with your baby.

DID YOU KNOW?
Babies will often respond to music they heard in the womb, such as the theme from your favourite soap!

Ready for more?

Sit on the floor with your baby facing you. Hold their shoulders and rock gently from side to side. Chant quietly:

'Side to side, here we go, stopping now to say hello.'

Stop rocking, say 'Hello', and carry on.

Hello, goodbye
learning about greetings

What you need:
- a favourite teddy bear (or other soft toy)
- a blanket
- a toy cot (or cardboard box)

WHAT TO DO:

1. Sit on a blanket on the floor with your baby.

2. Hold the teddy or toy behind your back and slowly bring it round to where baby can see it. Say 'Hello teddy' (or whatever the toy is called).

3. Play with the teddy and after a little while say 'Bye bye, teddy'. Move the teddy round behind your back.

4. Keep this teddy or toy special. Encourage your baby to hug and look after it.

Another idea: When you've finished playing, stroke the teddy together and tell baby, 'Time for teddy to sleep.' Together put teddy to bed in the cot and cover it up.

DID YOU KNOW?
Young babies have poor vision but learn to recognise their parents' faces very quickly.

Ready for more?

Give your baby a small blanket to put on the teddy in his bed.

Encourage baby to fetch 'Special Ted', before saying goodbye and putting it in the cot.

What is your baby learning?

This activity will help your baby develop the social skills of greeting and saying goodbye. Most children find that having a special toy gives important feelings of security.

HELPFUL HINTS

A soft, 'beanie' type teddy will be easier for a young baby to hold.

Help your baby uncurl his or her fingers by rubbing gently on the backs of their hands.

HELPFUL HINTS

To provide an extra reward, use a soft toy that squeaks when you squeeze it.

If your baby is younger, make sure his or her head is well supported.

What is your baby learning?

This activity will help with listening and will encourage attention. It also develops turn taking.

Do you mean me?
looking, smiling and responding to their name

DID YOU KNOW?

Newborn babies can't hear well. The middle ear of a newborn is full of fluid. Keep talking!

What you need:
- a teddy bear or other favourite soft toy

WHAT TO DO:

1. Hold your baby facing you on your knee. Sit so you can look into each other's faces at baby's eye level.

2. Tickle your baby's cheek gently and sing, *'Hello (baby's name), hello (baby's name), hello, hello, hello'.*

3. Take one of your baby's hands gently to your face and sing the rhyme again, using your own name in place of your baby's name.

Ready for more?

Sing the hello song while smiling and waving to your baby in a mirror.

4. Do this a couple of times. Then hold the teddy close and help your baby to hold or pat the teddy. Sing, *'Hello teddy, hello teddy, hello, hello hello.'*

5. Give your baby plenty of time, attention and smiles. Imitate any sounds they make and encourage them to look at you or the teddy as you sing each part of the rhyme.

Another idea: Vary the pace, or use funny voices and whispers to grab their attention.

Again, again!
asking for more

What you need:
- *a jar of bubble mixture and a blower*
- *some feathers (see the hint below)*

WHAT TO DO:

1. Sit opposite your baby so that your faces are level.

2. Call his or her name, then gently blow some bubbles so that they float close. Make sure they don't go into baby's face. Say 'Pop' and gently reach up and pop the bubbles. Pause for a moment and wait for them to make a sound, reach out or gesture to request more.

3. Say, 'Again?' and wait for a sound, word, or gesture. Repeat, 'Again?' and blow some more bubbles. Allow plenty of time for your baby to show you they want you to do it again.

4. Play the same game with the feathers, blowing them high into the air and waiting for them to float down, before asking, 'Again?'

Another idea: Play the game with squares of tissue or transparent paper.

Ready for more?

Build towers of bricks and knock them down. Let your baby join in. Encourage sounds, words or gestures to mean 'Again' each time the tower is knocked down.

Play a favourite tickle game and then ask your baby, 'Again?'

What is your baby learning?

This activity helps to develop the notion of cause and effect. It's also important in linking actions with sounds (the start of talking). Is your baby using sounds and gestures? Looking? Reaching?

HELPFUL HINTS
Very young babies have trouble following things that move quickly. Give them plenty of time to try and reach for the bubble and ask 'Again?'.

Peek-a-boo
smiles and surprises

What you need:

- small (roughly 30cm²) squares of fabrics with different textures – net, fur, wool, etc.
- a blanket

Ready for more?

Try hiding noisy toys under the fabric. Can you find them together?

Put the blanket over the head of a doll or soft toy. Play peek-a-boo. Encourage your baby to pull off the cloth when you say 'boo'.

WHAT TO DO:

1. Give your baby time to pat, pull and explore the fabrics. Experience the sensation of feeling them on yours and your baby's cheeks, fingers and toes.

2. Hold out a hand in a 'Give it to me' gesture and say, 'Thank you'. Gently take the fabric, hold it up to your face and play peek-a-boo.

3. Each time you play let your baby choose the fabric.

4. Spread out the blanket. Hold it up and play peek-a-boo. Hold it high in the air and encourage your baby to come under the blanket with you. Snuggle up under the blanket and play peek-a-boo with a corner. Encourage eye contact by rewarding with smiles and lots of attention.

Another idea: Play peek-a-boo round the edge of a door.

HELPFUL HINTS

Playing 'peek-a-boo' with a rattle or shaker will help a young baby to locate it.

Don't hurry this game. Allow plenty of time for repetition.

What is your baby learning?

This activity helps develop listening and understanding, and is good preparation for your baby's first words.

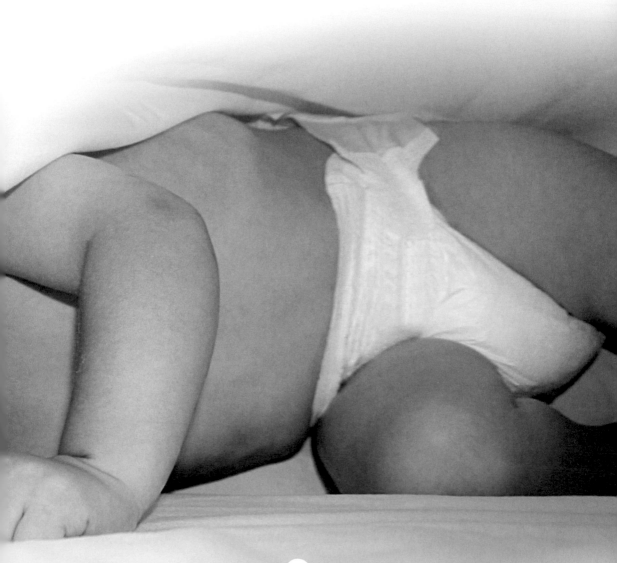

Up and down
moving and singing

What you need:
- *No special equipment for this activity.*

WHAT TO DO:

1. Hold your baby in your arms or under their arms so you are face to face.

2. Look into your baby's eyes and say, 'Hello (baby's name), hello (baby's name). Shall we play a game?'

3. Lift your baby gently up and down and say,
'Here we go up, up, up.
Here we go down, down, down.' Use a simple tune or a sing-song voice. Smile as you talk.

4. Do this a couple of times.

5. Look at your baby all the time you are playing this game. Imitate any sounds baby makes and encourage them to look at you as you sing.

Another idea: Sit your baby in your lap and play the game with a soft toy, lifting it up and down.

Ready for more?

Babies love this game, and some like to be lifted quite vigorously. Play the game standing up, so the feeling of up and down is greater.

Encourage baby to play the game with a toy.

What is your baby learning?

This activity helps to develop listening and attending, and promotes the idea of taking turns. See if you can spot your baby turning to the sound and showing anticipation.

HELPFUL HINTS
Whisper or use a funny voice to get and keep your baby's attention.
Remember that young babies need their head supported when you're playing physical games.

DID YOU
KNOW?
*Touching helps
your baby to grow
by stimulating
growth-promoting
hormones.*

What is your baby learning?

This helps to develop copying and making sounds and encourages taking turns.

Echo, echo
copying sounds and expressions

What you need:
- *No special equipment for this activity.*

WHAT TO DO:

1. Sit with your baby in your lap, so your faces are level. If your baby is very young, keep your face close (about 20–25cm is best).

2. Call your baby's name or talk to them to get their attention.

3. Use exaggerated expressions and a lively voice to maintain their interest.

4. Now use different facial expressions and sounds to encourage your baby to watch and copy you. Try slowly poking your tongue out, opening your mouth wide, 'popping' your lips, blowing out your cheeks, etc.

Ready for more?

With older babies make the expressions more complicated.

Play the game in a mirror so that baby can see themselves and you.

5. Be patient. Small babies have to work hard at copying you – their muscles are immature. Praise any response!

Another idea: Play this game at changing time.

DID YOU KNOW?

Babies have a natural tendency to copy. Learning to copy is essential to early learning.

Googling
exchanging sounds and noises

What you need:
- *No special equipment for this activity.*

Ready for more?

Older babies and children love echo games. Try some simple 'My turn, your turn' songs or rhymes.

Try passing an object as you make the sound, e.g. a small soft toy or rattle.

WHAT TO DO:

1. Sit with your baby in your lap, facing you and near enough to see your face.

2. Call baby's name to attract their attention.

3. When you have her/his attention make a short repetitive sound – goo-goo, ma-ma, da-da, la-la, na-na, and so on.

4. Wait for your baby to respond. If they don't, make the sound again and wait for a response. Praise any response they make, even if it isn't the same sound as you made (it probably won't be).

5. Keep going, taking turns, exchanging smiles as well as sounds.

6. Stop when your baby loses concentration or interest.

Another idea: Let baby start the exchange and copy sounds they make.

What is your baby learning?

This game helps to develop concentration and taking turns, and leads to first words. Watch your baby to see them copying, using their voice, watching you.

HELPFUL HINTS

If your baby is still very young remember to stay close. They won't see you properly if you're more than about 25cm away.

Give your baby plenty of time to respond – it may take several goes for them to get the idea.

DID YOU KNOW?

Babies communicate physically before they can communicate verbally and they quickly learn key gestures.

Copy cat
copying facial expressions

What you need:

- *a few moments of one-to-one quiet time*
- *a comfortable place to sit with your baby*

Ready for more?

Sing rhymes and songs to your baby, tapping the rhythm gently on their tummy or back.

Play anticipation games, such as 'I'm coming to tickle you'.

WHAT TO DO:

1. Hold your baby and support his or head so that you can easily look into their face.

2. Remember that young babies focus best around 25cm. Make sure you are close enough for your baby to be able to see you clearly.

3. Sing hello to your baby. Stroke their cheeks and gently engage their attention. Pause, then stick out your tongue. Repeat this every 20 seconds or so. Keep going for about two minutes to give baby plenty of time to respond by copying your action.

4. Reward *any* response by smiling and praising.

Another idea: Try some different actions, such as twitching your nose, smiling and so on. Repeat the action for one to two minutes to give baby plenty of time to copy.

What is your baby learning?

This helps to develop attention and listening skills and promotes turn taking. Watch for your baby looking, listening, responding and copying actions.

Fingers and toes
fun with finger puppets

What you need:
- *some fur fabric (bright green would be good, but any colour will do)*
- *fabric glue or a simple sewing kit*
- *scissors*

Ready for more?

Put your baby's hands between your own and rub them gently, singing 'Rub-a-dub dub, rub-a-dub dub.'

Lie your baby on her or his back, hold their ankles in the air and play 'peek-a-boo' between their feet.

WHAT TO DO:

1. Make a very simple green caterpillar finger puppet to fit your index finger. Use fabric glue or stitches to fix the sides.

2. Make sure that your baby is well supported, perhaps sitting sideways on your knee so that you can look into each other's eyes.

3. Try this new finger rhyme, gradually wriggling and creeping the finger puppet up baby's arm into the palm of their hand, round and round and then down their arm, tummy, legs to their toes:

   Wriggle, wriggle, here I come, caterpillar on my thumb

   Round and round, off he goes, all the way down to my toes.

Another idea: Start the rhyme very slowly, and pause before running your fingers down to baby's toes for a gentle tickle.

What is your baby learning?

This helps to develop attention, listening skills and understanding. It leads to babbling and from that to first words.

Almost ballroom
slaves to the rhythm

DID YOU KNOW?
Most babies enjoy music and it can develop brain power.

What you need:
- *No special equipment for this activity.*

WHAT TO DO:

1. Hold your baby comfortably in your arms, facing you.

2. Move around in a circle, taking side steps and singing

   Step and step, 1, 2, 3, step and step, dance with me,
   Step and step, 1, 2, 3, step and stop, look at me!

3. On the last line stop suddenly and swing baby smoothly high in the air and hold them there. Hold their eye contact for a moment before lowering them gently down again and continuing the dance.

Another idea: If you have a friend who also has a baby it's great fun to get them to join in. The babies will enjoy being together and watching each other.

Ready for more?

Get an older child or your partner to sit on the floor opposite you. Pat a beach ball or balloon between you.

Find a hat and take it in turns putting it on the baby, taking it off, then on you and taking it off. This is another game where it's good to have an older child or a partner to join in.

What is your baby learning?

This game helps anticipation, the enjoyment of repetition, and concentration. Watch your baby to see if he or she is feeling the rhythm and moving with you, sharing fun, showing trust and anticipation.

HELPFUL HINTS

You can be livelier with older children, but for small babies go gently and make sure they have good enough head control before you play this sort of game.

Most babies love this game but if your baby doesn't, stop at once, and don't worry. They simply might not be ready for it yet.

Eye to eye
singing and rocking

What you need:
- *a few moments of one-to-one quiet time*
- *a comfortable place to sit with your baby*

WHAT TO DO:

1. Every baby needs the opportunity for quiet conversations and this game is to encourage them.

2. Hold your baby with his or her head well supported so that you can look at their face easily and they can see you.

3. Remember that young babies focus best at around 25cm. Make sure you are close enough for your baby to be able to see you clearly.

4. Sing a simple nursery rhyme or song as you gently rock backwards and forwards. Take it slowly – remember, babies need time to focus and follow.

5. Talk quietly to your baby as you rock. Encourage and praise them as they move their faces, hands and bodies.

Ready for more?

Each time you change or feed your baby, talk to them and make eye contact.

Sing lots of rhymes and songs to your baby, looking at them as you sing.

Another idea: Look, smile, wait for the baby to smile back. Praise them. Try again, smile again, praise again.

What is your baby learning?

This activity develops attention and listening skills and encourages responding and taking turns. It is good preparation for learning to converse.

HELPFUL HINTS

When deciding where to sit, choose somewhere where the light is falling on your face so your baby can see you easily.

Some children find the rocking soothing, others will respond better if you keep still. Try both and see which your baby prefers.

HELPFUL HINTS

An expressive voice and slightly higher tone will attract your baby's attention and engage them in the game.

Show your baby the toy before you start the game, so they know what to expect. Sometimes stop in the middle of a song, pause and gasp to grab attention.

Here comes teddy
hide and find fun

What you need:
- a small teddy or soft toy

WHAT TO DO:

1. This game is about listening and anticipation, taking meaning from the tone of your voice.

2. Prop your baby securely in a baby chair or on a cushion. If your baby is very young, make sure they have good head support.

3. Kneel or sit facing baby, so they can see your face and what you are doing.

4. Using a lively and enthusiastic tone say:

   Here comes teddy (or rabbit or whatever), here he comes,
   Along your legs and up to your tum!

6. Walk the toy up the baby's legs and tummy as you talk.

7. Praise any response and indication of 'again'.

Another idea: Make the toy appear from different places, such as behind you, behind baby, from under a blanket.

Ready for more?

Play other simple games of anticipation such as 'Round and Round the Garden' or 'I'm Coming to Tickle You!'

Play these 'wait for it' games at changing time.

What is your baby learning?

This game develops attention, listening skills and understanding, and stimulates first words. Watch your baby to see if they are watching, responding (gurgling, looking excited, waving limbs), and showing anticipation.

DID YOU
KNOW?
Newborn babies can recognise the natural scent (pheromones) from their mother's body.

Which one?
it's your choice

DID YOU KNOW? Choosing is complicated and young babies will simply go for the strongest colours or shape.

What you need:
- a warm, comfortable familiar place
- a basket of small toys and other objects, easy for your baby to hold

WHAT TO DO:

1. Sit opposite your baby. Make sure that they are supported.

2. Pick up two of the toys or objects and hold them where baby can reach out for them. Say in a sing-song voice:

   Which one would you like to have?
   Take the one you'd like to have.

3. Watch for a response to one or the other, and encourage your baby to take the toy in their hand. Name the objects as you offer them. Talk aloud about what you are doing.

4. Let your baby play with the object for a while before holding out two more objects. Praise reaching and holding.

Another idea: Play the game with objects that make a sound, or are brightly coloured.

Ready for more?

Offer your baby choices as soon as they can hold something. Try finger foods, pieces of fabric, small soft toys.

Whenever you are with your baby, talk about what you are doing. Continue, even if they don't respond.

What is your baby learning?

This activity is good preparation for learning to name things, and will help to lay the groundwork for conversations.

HELPFUL HINTS

Make sure you have baby's attention before you offer them objects to choose.

Older babies can cope with a larger number of choices so they feel a sense of control and partnership.

Feely stuff
exploring fabrics

What you need:

- pieces of fabric with different textures – e.g. fur, wool, plastic, leather, denim, fleece, cotton, net (If you don't have any fabric you could use items of clothing with different textures.)

WHAT TO DO:

1. Choose a piece of fabric. Put it on your baby's arm, leg, hand, cheek, fingers or toes.

2. Stroke your baby's skin gently with the fabric.

3. Talk about the feel of the fabric, using simple words such as 'soft', 'smooth', 'shiny', 'tickly'. Your baby might like it if you make it into a little sing-song chant.

4. Encourage baby to hold the fabric with two hands.

5. Try helping your baby to bring the fabric towards their face.

6. Change to a new fabric when baby seems ready.

Another idea: Put your baby on different fabrics when they lie on the floor.

Ready for more?

Encourage your baby to do the choosing, selecting the fabric and feeling it on their skin. If the piece is big enough, join in!

Gently put a piece of fabric over baby's head (and yours). Play peep-bo!

What is your baby learning?

This activity leads to imitating and comparing.

HELPFUL HINTS

Start with one or two textures. Allow plenty of time to explore and enjoy each texture. Watch carefully for likes and dislikes.

Stroking the cheek with fabric or a feather is a very soothing sensation for most babies and for many older children, and has a calming effect.

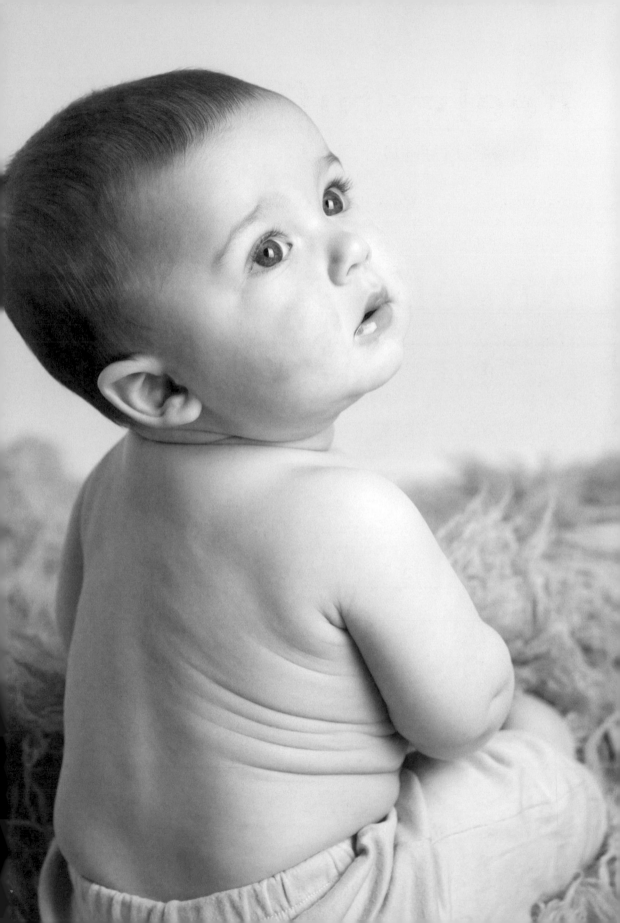

Angel's Delight
messy play on reflective surfaces

What you need:

- a safety mirror or a large shiny metal tray or tin lid
- mousse or thick yoghurt
- an aerosol can of UHT cream

WHAT TO DO:

1. Spoon some mousse on to the mirror, tray or tin lid.

2. Sit beside your baby and play together, patting and prodding the mousse. Encourage baby to trail her/his fingers through the foam, squeezing it, prodding it and rolling it between their hands.

3. Add some cream and encourage your baby to use two hands together to mix the cream and mousse.

4. Give a simple commentary on what he or she is doing, using single words and short phrases. Comment on changes, such as 'more', 'all gone' or 'stirring'. Encourage new actions.

Another idea: Add plastic scourers and washing up brushes. Encourage exploration of up and down and circular movements.

DID YOU KNOW?
Some babies' eyes change colour as their bodies start to produce melanin.

Ready for more?

Draw circles and lines in the mousse.

Tape bubble wrap to a table top so that it covers it. Spread the mousse and cream mixture over the bubble wrap and explore how it feels.

What is your baby learning?

This encourages exploration and investigation and starts to develop the movement and control needed for writing.

Lay it on the line
a line of things to feel

What you need:
- *lots of different surfaces and textures: pieces of fabric, corrugated card, bubble wrap, pegs, a glove, some big beads or buttons, etc.*
- *string or wool*
- *a washing line*

WHAT TO DO:

1. Sit your baby in a seat or prop them up with a cushion where they can easily see you.

2. Tie a piece of washing line or cord between two chairs. Using small bits of string or wool, attach some of the things you have collected to the line.

3. Talk about what you are doing as you do it, and name the things you are tying on the line.

4. When you have about six different things fixed on the line move your baby to where they can reach it.

5. Encourage him or her to reach out for and grasp the things on the line. Talk and listen.

Another idea: Attach several strings to a washing line or cord and fix it above the changing table, or across your baby's cot or buggy.

Ready for more?

Make a portable toy by threading moving pieces on a trainer or boot lace.

Try a line of things that make sounds, such as bells, shells, rattles, or small toys.

What is your baby learning?

This activity helps with the foundations for investigating and exploring, as well as describing things.

SAFETY NOTE: Do not leave small babies alone with strings. They could become entangled in them.

HELPFUL HINTS

Make sure that baby is in a good light when they are exploring.

Find out which textures baby seems to like and talk about these. Allow them plenty of time.

Spots or stripes
exploring pattern and texture

What you need:

- a collection of everyday objects with spots, stripes, slots and holes (e.g. a tea strainer, draining spoon, spaghetti measurer, biscuit cutters, stripy tea towel)
- a tray

Ready for more?

Try cutting holes and slits in old pieces of fabric to poke hands through.

Explore hair scrunchies, bangles and bracelets together. Make a collection of card and plastic tubes to explore.

WHAT TO DO:

1. Clear a space and remove any objects that might be distracting.

2. Make sure your baby is sitting in a well-supported position.

3. Offer your baby one of the objects from your collection. Encourage reaching, grasping and holding with two hands.

4. Explore the object together. Hold it up and look at it. Let your baby handle it. Try gently touching your baby's hands or feet with it. Feel the holes, peep through the slots, touch the spots. Talk all the time, naming the object and telling your baby about. Don't worry that your baby won't understand you – it's the act of communicating and describing that's important.

5. Change to a new thing when you judge that baby is ready to move on. Allow plenty of time to explore the tray of objects without interruption. Stay with baby while they explore.

Another idea: Put on a hat or a pair of glasses and try the same activity again.

DID YOU KNOW?

Babies can make out colours from about 2 weeks. They prefer strong colours and bigger patterns.

What is your baby learning?

This activity helps with making choices, reaching and investigating.

HELPFUL HINTS

Your baby might need you to take their hand(s) gently to the objects.

If your baby clenches her/his fists, gently tickle the back of the hands to help them open them up.

Squeeze and prod
making changes

What you need:

- small quantities of cooked sticky rice, mashed potato, jelly
- small plastic bowls and cups
- small plastic trays, freezer box lids, plant trays, etc.

Ready for more?

Make small, sticky rice balls and hold them out so baby can reach for and grasp them.

Provide a slotted spoon or plastic potato masher so that baby can pound, mix and poke.

WHAT TO DO:

1. Make sure that your baby is sitting well supported in a baby chair and dressed (or undressed!) ready for messy play.

2. Sit opposite your baby and place a small quantity of sticky rice on their tray. Pat it, prod it and then gently squeeze some through your own fingers. Encourage them to feel it.

3. Help your baby to squeeze it, poke it through your fingers and so on. Cup your hand for them to poke some rice in.

4. Give plenty of uninterrupted time and attention. Encourage your baby to pat and rub the rice with both hands.

5. Do the same with the mashed potato and then with the jelly. You could mix them all together for a very messy medley!

Another idea: Try some very soft bread dough as an alternative.

What is your baby learning?

This activity helps develops fine motor control and leads to understanding cause and effect.

HELPFUL HINTS

Your baby may be wary of such new textures. Don't worry if they are – just introduce them slowly.

Give baby as much time as they need – they may prefer to watch you first.

The string's the thing
fun with strings and ribbons

What you need:
- ribbons (several different colours if possible)
- scissors
- plastic bangles
- small shakers, bells and rattles

WHAT TO DO:

1. Cut several pieces of ribbon, each about 30cm long.

2. Tie a plastic bangle to each cut length of ribbon. Tie a rattle, shaker or bell(s) to the other end of each ribbon. Check that all is secure.

3. Sit your baby in a well-supported position.

4. Place one of the shakers on the floor or on a tray in front of your baby. Offer them the bangle to hold. Help them to grasp it if they need you to.

5. Talk and sing to your baby as they explore the bangle. Gently tug the ribbon and shaker towards them, and encourage them to try to pull it. Reward any attempt to pull by smiling and saying 'Again?'

Ready for more?

Use different textures and types of string and ribbon attached to different sound makers.

Fix a plastic spoon to a ribbon as an alternative type of handle.

Another idea: Put the items on a tin tray. This will make a good noise as they are pulled and dropped.

What is your baby learning?

This leads to exploring and to understanding cause and effect.

What is your baby learning?

*This activity helps your baby to
learn to use fingers and hands to
investigate and make marks. It also
presents the idea that things are still
there even if you can't see them.*

All steamed up!
first marks

What you need:

• *a mirror or
window*

Ready for more?

Use a small hand
mirror for the same
game.

Play the game at
changing or bath
time.

WHAT TO DO:

1. Hold your baby in your arms and stand very near
the window or mirror, so you can both see. Talk to
your baby all the time as you look at each other in
the mirror.

2. Gently breathe on the window or mirror, so a
small patch of the glass mists up. Say, 'Look, all
gone!' as your faces disappear.

3. Make sure that your baby is looking at the
misty mirror. Now clear the small patch away
with your hand.

4. Greet your baby in the mirror again.

5. Now breathe on a different part
of the mirror or window and
draw a smiling face in the
mist.

Another idea: Get up really
close and let your baby pat the
mirror so they make marks
too.

DID YOU KNOW?
Reading to your
baby increases sensitivity
to the sounds of
language, and helps
bonding.

Hold It
touching and exploring

What you need:
- pieces of gift ribbon, string or cord
- small and interesting objects such as clean feathers, beads, small bells, etc

WHAT TO DO:

1. Cut some lengths of string or ribbon and tie one of the objects on the end of each.

2. Sit your baby facing you in a chair or securely supported on a rug or mat.

3. Choose one of the strings and dangle the object in front of baby, just within reach of their outstretched arms but not too close.

4. Keep the object as still as you can, so your baby can focus on it.

5. Talk to your baby and encourage them to reach out for the object. Lower the string so baby can pull the object towards them.

6. Try again with a different object.

Another idea: Hang strings above the changing area. Change the objects every few days.

Ready for more?

Make a simple mobile and hang it where baby can see it when they are lying down.

Hang old CDs in trees and bushes in your garden or on a balcony, where baby can watch them spinning and shining.

What is your baby learning?

This activity helps your baby to practise focusing their eyes and leads to grabbing and holding, which in turn develops hand control.

HELPFUL HINTS

A pillow or cushion each side of a young baby may help them to lie still and concentrate.

Brightly coloured objects and things that make sounds will add interest and help baby to stay interested.

HELPFUL HINTS

Tape some small bells to the back of the card.
Shake the card gently to help baby focus and
look in the direction of the sound.

Try with your baby in a relaxer or car seat and
hang the cards from a string slung between two
dining chairs.

DID YOU
KNOW?

*Contrasting patterns
help babies learn
to focus. They like
chequer boards and
spotty fabrics.*

Reach for it
black and white patterns

What you need:
- *white card*
- *black card (or
  paper)*
- *scissors, glue
  and ribbon*
- *a hoop or baby
  gym*

Ready for more?

Cut out eyes, noses
and mouths to make
black and white face
patterns.

Add shiny borders to
the cards.

WHAT TO DO:

1. Cut some different shapes from the black card.
Try zigzags, circles, triangles, squares, blobs. Glue
them to the white card to make black and white
contrasting patterns. Make different patterns on
each side of the white card.

2. Tie the cards securely to the
hoop or baby gym. Lay your
baby under the baby gym or
hang the hoop securely over
their cot so that the cards are
within easy reach.

3. Tap the cards and
encourage your baby to
look at them and to reach
out for and pat them.

Another idea: Try tiny
black and white spots
or a chess board pattern.

What is your
baby learning?

*As well as
strengthening the
muscles needed to
focus the eyes, this
helps to develop
the co-ordination
of the muscles
needed for
grabbing and
holding.*

Look up
soothing sights

What you need:

- *some simple mobiles: black and white or reflective (if you don't have any it's easy to make one by hanging objects from a plastic coat hanger)*
- *a rug for your baby to lie on and a nest of cushions*

WHAT TO DO:

1. Make sure that your baby is warm and comfortable, lying on the rug. Enclose the space with cushions. Hang the mobiles above baby, so they can gaze and focus on them.

2. The mobiles should be close enough for your baby to be able to see them clearly (remember that young babies focus best around 25cm). Check that the mobiles are fixed securely and if baby pats them they will not become entangled.

3. Move the mobiles gently and talk to your baby, getting them to look towards the mobiles. Hum a gentle tune, encouraging baby to track the mobile from side to side.

   Another idea: Put your baby on his or her tummy and roll brightly coloured or noisy toys from side to side for them to focus on.

Ready for more?

Use glitter sticks or bubble tubes to encourage looking and reaching.

Shine a torch on to a wall for baby to follow the beam (sit beside them so you don't accidentally shine it into their eyes).

What is your baby learning?

This activity helps looking and tracking, develops attention and is a good starter for sensory play.

HELPFUL HINTS

Roll up two small towels and place one each side of a small baby to give them extra support and comfort.

Experiment by holding the mobiles in different positions to see where baby can most easily focus.

Pumpkin pie
truly messy play!

What you need:

- a pumpkin
- a sharp knife and chopping board
- a pan and access to a stove or hob
- a potato masher, milk

WHAT TO DO:

1. Peel the pumpkin carefully and chop it into even-sized chunks. Boil it for 25 minutes, then drain. Add some cold milk and mash to a smooth consistency. Leave until cool.

2. Make sure your baby is sitting well-supported in a chair or on your knee. Take some of the mashed pumpkin and squeeze it through your fingers. Give baby the chance to smell and feel the texture.

3. Encourage your baby to touch your hands and pat at the mashed pumpkin. Hold their hands gently in yours and, if they are enjoying the experience, rub hands together gently, exploring the texture of the mashed pumpkin.

   Another idea: Place the mashed pumpkin for a few hours in the fridge and play with it again. This will give a very different sensation.

Ready for more?

Try gently isolating index fingers and poking them deep into the mash.

Pour a little water over the mash and explore the changing textures. Add a small wooden spoon to bash the mashed pumpkin!

What is your baby learning?

As well as being great fun, this helps lay the foundations for creativity, develops concentration and investigation and leads to sensory play.

HELPFUL HINTS

Most babies will put the mashed pumpkin into their mouths. Play this game after a meal when they are not hungry.

Shiver and shake!
exploring vibration

What you need:
- *massage rollers*
- *toys that shake or vibrate*
- *a balloon*
- *a drum or tambourine*

WHAT TO DO:

1. Sit with your baby well supported, so you can gaze easily into each other's faces. Gently tap baby's hands and lower arms with your fingertips. Sing 'Tap, tap, tap' – pause – 'Tap, tap, tap' – stop.

2. Next give him or her the massage roller to feel. Help them to hold it in both hands, and to feel it on fingertips, palms, backs of hands. Very gently roll it up your baby's forearms.

3. Watch carefully to see how your baby responds to the unfamiliar sensations.

4. Try touching the vibrating toys, and tapping the balloon together, or put your baby's hands on the drum or tambourine as you tap the edges to make it vibrate.

Another idea: Fix ribbons tightly across a tray top. Ping the ribbons.

What is your baby learning?

Exploring vibrations helps lay the foundations for creativity and leads to shared fun and sensory play.

Ready for more?

Try the vibrating toys and massage rollers on legs, feet and toes.

Support your baby on top of a large exercise ball or space hopper. Lightly tap the sides of the ball and feel the vibrations.

DID YOU
KNOW?
Babies are sensitive to vibration which may, remind them of sensations they experienced in the womb.

DID YOU KNOW?

Babies and toddlers are, pound for pound, stronger than horses. This is especially true of their legs.

Bubble trouble
something in the air

What you need:

- *bubbles and a blower*

WHAT TO DO:

1. Make sure that your baby is sitting or propped in a well-supported position, near a flat surface – e.g. a changing table, a wall, a low table, a tray or a baby chair with a table.

2. Sit opposite your baby and gently blow some bubbles towards them, being careful not to blow them in their face.

3. Try to blow the bubbles near their hands, so they can feel them popping and can touch and reach for them.

4. Now blow some bubbles so they land on the flat surface. Put your hand out and pat or poke some of the bubbles. Encourage baby to reach out and pat the bubbles as they land too.

Another idea: Try blowing bubbles at changing time. Your baby will love the feeling of them landing and bursting on their tummy.

Ready for more?

Put some very bubbly washing up liquid foam on a tray and encourage your baby to pat and feel it.

Fill a small fabric or plastic bag with crinkly paper, cooked pasta or rice. Make sure the bag is sealed properly.

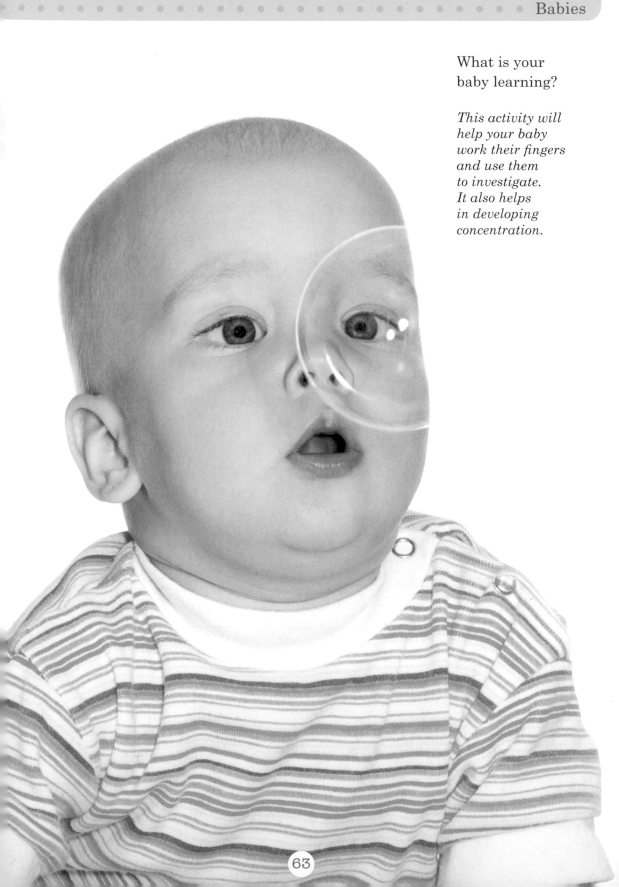

What is your
baby learning?

*This activity will
help your baby
work their fingers
and use them
to investigate.
It also helps
in developing
concentration.*

Feel the difference
texture and treasure

DID YOU
KNOW?
Grasping and holding are reflexes. Babies hang on to things instinctively but have to learn to let go.

What you need:
- a shallow plastic tray
- a selection of objects with a range of textures – crinkly paper, a woolly sock, furry glove, toothbrush, hard plastic cup, etc.

WHAT TO DO:

1. Make a 'treasure tray' by placing some of the objects on the tray (not too many).

2. Pick up one object and tap it on the tray to get your baby's attention.

3. Talk and sing to your baby. Help them to explore the objects.

4. Try rubbing the different textures firmly but gently on the backs of their hands.

5. Encourage your baby to reach for and pat the objects with two hands.

6. Reward their efforts at reaching with words of praise, cuddles, gentle strokes and tickles.

Another idea: Try patting warm, damp, bubbly sponges.

Ready for more?

Put together a tray of wooden objects with different textures to pat.

Offer the objects one at a time for baby to grasp and hold.

What is your baby learning?

This activity helps to develop the co-ordination and muscles needed for grasping and holding, shaking and letting go.

HELPFUL HINTS

Make sure that your baby is well supported. It is hard to reach and pat objects if you are still working on your sitting balance! If the highchair is too wide for your baby you can use a small cushion or rolled up tea towel next to them to help hold them firm.

HELPFUL HINTS

Give baby suitable objects to feel before using them. For example, help them to feel their vest before putting it on, or the flannel before washing.

Some babies need lots of encouragement to reach and grab. Try reflective objects, such as a baby mirror. Tie bells to it to make it even more interesting.

What is your baby learning?

This activity helps develop the notion of cause and effect and supports the development of fine motor control.

Grab that
sticks and shakers

What you need:
- *rattles*
- *shakers (use bought ones, or make your own with dried beans, beads, rice, etc.)*
- *small wooden spoons*
- *ribbons*

Ready for more?

Hold the shakers on alternate sides so baby can practise reaching to the side.

Provide a plastic bowl full of ribbons or scarves to reach for, grab and explore.

WHAT TO DO:

1. Sit opposite your baby and hold the rattle out so they can reach for it. Hold it in the mid-line so they can see it easily.

2. Shake the rattle, call their name and gently lift their arm from the elbow towards the rattle or shaker. Help them to grasp the rattle and shake it. Share their enjoyment of the sound.

3. Tie the ribbons together in a bundle. Trail them through your baby's outstretched hands. Encourage them to grasp the ribbons, or gently twine the ribbons over both hands.

4. Offer your baby the wooden spoon to grab and hold. Hold the spoon with them and sing, 'Shake, shake, shake; Tap, tap, tap'.

Another idea: Chiffon scarves are great for reaching and grabbing.

DID YOU KNOW?
Babies get some protection from infection from their mothers. This is increased by breastfeeding.

65

HELPFUL HINTS

Some babies need you to start by covering your face only as far as your eyes, so they are sure you are still there.

When your baby is in her or his stroller push them gently away from you, then pull them back towards you with a 'Boo'.

What is your baby learning?

This activity helps to develop the notion of absence/ presence and stimulates remembering. It also encourages joining in.

Now you see me
disappearing and reappearing

What you need:

- *a cover – e.g. a cloth, towel, blanket or sheet*

WHAT TO DO:

1. You can play this game in many places - on the changing table or mat, in a baby chair, during feeding, or when you are having a quiet cuddle.

2. Call your baby's name softly to attract their attention.

3. Hold the cover in front of your face and slowly draw it down so your face appears. Don't move too quickly with a young baby or they won't be able to follow what is happening. As your face appears, smile and speak gently.

4. Very young babies may not like the 'BOO' bit to start with, so make sure you respond to their reactions and take it gently.

Another idea: Let your baby surprise you by putting the cover very gently over their face and letting them pull it off.

Ready for more?

As they get used to this game, most babies enjoy the predicted surprise of 'BOO' as you reappear.

Try putting the cover right over your head and letting baby pull it off.

DID YOU KNOW?

It takes young babies a long time to understand that things are still there when they can't see them.

Look at me!
a face to face game

DID YOU KNOW?
The heart of a newborn baby beats between 130 and 160 times a minute, more than twice the rate of a normal adult.

What you need:
- *No special equipment for this activity.*

Ready for more?

Sing these little songs at changing time, or feeding time.

Use a face puppet or rattle to attract attention. Hold it near your face and move it when baby is looking at you.

WHAT TO DO:

1. Sit your baby in a chair or against a secure and comfortable prop.

2. Sit yourself opposite your baby.

3. Call your baby's name to attract their attention.

4. Sing or chant to your baby, *'Here I am, here I am, close to you. There you are, there you are, close to me'.* You could use the tune of 'Tommy Thumb' or make up your own.

5. As you sing, stroke your baby's hand or arm.

6. Sing the words again. You want your baby to respond, so praise any reaction (such as kicking, waving, smiling) by smiling and saying, 'Well done (baby's name), you are looking at me.'

Another idea: Sing the song holding your baby beside you and facing a mirror so you can both see each other and yourselves.

What is your baby learning?

Getting your baby to respond to you and you responding to them is preparation for the give and take of daily life, including learning to take part in conversations.

HELPFUL HINTS

Babies and small children need to feel physically secure. Make sure your baby is well supported wherever they are.

The sound of your voice is very reassuring to your baby. Talk to them a lot and sing to them often. (They'll enjoy it even if you're not very musical!)

There's nothing like a cuddle
feeling safe

What you need:
- *a fleece or baby blanket*
- *a soft toy or teddy (optional)*

WHAT TO DO:

1. Hold your baby in your lap or your arms.

2. Wrap the fleece or blanket round both of you, so you are together inside the warmth. Include the teddy or soft toy if you wish.

3. Hum or talk gently to your baby, repeating their name and singing lullaby songs so they feel really safe.

4. Stroke their arms, hands and back. Use sounds like 'shhh', 'lala', 'mmm' and slow, gentle speech.

5. Rocking gently will increase baby's feeling of security. Try not to fall asleep yourself!

Another idea: You could walk slowly around your home with your baby in the blanket, talking in a soft voice about what you see.

Ready for more?

Sit on a beanbag or floor cushion or in a soft chair with your baby (and an older brother or sister if you can), just watching their world and talking quietly about what you see. This will build their confidence in the safety and security of what goes on around them.

What is your baby learning?

This activity will help to develop confidence, calmness and the ability to relax.

HELPFUL HINTS

Try to spend a little time each day just holding and talking to your baby. Relax and enjoy some cuddles at the end of the day.

Stroking soft or furry fabrics can be very relaxing, but small babies will need help with this.

Happy hands
hands together and to the face

What you need:

- *a wrist toy or elastic hair scrunchie*

Ready for more?

Put the wrist toy or bells on your baby's ankle and play again, singing 'Happy Feet'.

As your baby develops introduce some clapping games to encourage them to bring their two hands together and clap.

DID YOU KNOW?

Learning to clap is an important step in developing physical co-ordination.

WHAT TO DO:

1. Sit opposite your baby or with him/her on your knee, or if your baby is very young put them on their back on a soft rug. If he or she is a wriggler place a rolled up blanket on either side so they can focus on their hands rather than their escape!

2. Gently bring your babies hands together in the mid-line and sing:

   Happy hands, happy hands
   Touch it, feel it, happy hands

3. You can use the tune of 'Jack and Jill' or make one up.

4. Tap baby's hands together gently. Encourage them to feel and shake the wrist toy. Give them plenty of time for unhurried and uninterrupted exploration.

5. Sing the song again, and this time gently help your baby bring their hands together in the mid-line and then up to their face so that they can gaze at their hands.

Another idea: Make up some more songs for simple hand games.

What is your baby learning?

This will help your baby learn to clap, pat and reach.

HELPFUL HINTS

Wrist toys are useful for encouraging young babies to lie still at changing time.
Vary the pace of the song or use a funny voice to grab baby's attention.

HELPFUL HINTS

Try some different patting, on sponges and flannels at bath time, or on a slab of pastry when you are cooking. Encourage an older baby to isolate their index finger and poke the mat.

What is your baby learning?

Exploration is the theme of this activity, which helps children find out about objects, the materials they're made of and how they behave.

Pat the mat
fun with pat mats

What you need:
- *black and white fabric*
- *stick-on Velcro or a simple sewing kit*
- *scraps of crunchy or crinkly paper for filling*

WHAT TO DO:

1. Make a simple bag shape, using the Velcro or sewing straight seams for the edges. Fill the bag with scraps of crunchy or crinkly paper. Seal it securely with Velcro or by stitching it.

2. Put the mat on a flat surface and encourage your baby to pat the mat, using two hands together. Talk and sing as baby pats the mat.

3. Copy your baby's actions and say or chant 'Pat, pat, pat'. Vary your voice to get and keep baby's attention.

4. Try big, slow movements alternated with quick, tiny pats.

Another idea: Fill the bag with soft sponge or feathers. Add some squeakers for new appeal.

Ready for more?

For an older or more mobile baby make a giant stamping mat with just a little filling.

Noisy toys, bells and squeakers in the bag will keep the fun going.

DID YOU KNOW?
Touch is important for learning. Children will often pat or slap things to explore them.

Feeling good
baby massage

What you need:
- *baby oil (apricot and avocado are both good)*
- *a changing mat*
- *a towel, blanket or shawl*

Ready for more?

Try back or tummy massages, with gentle, soothing stroking and smoothing.

Try the massage as baby is going to sleep at rest time, to help them to relax.

WHAT TO DO:

1. Choose a warm, quiet draught-free place for this activity. You can rest your baby on your lap or on a changing mat.

2. Sit on the carpet or a cushion, with your back supported by a wall. Put a warm towel on your lap or on the changing mat, and gently lie your baby on the towel.

3. Remove their shoes and any clothing on arms or legs.

4. Pour a little warmed oil on your hands and rub them together, talking to your baby all the time, maintaining eye contact and telling them in a quiet voice what you are doing.

5. Now gently massage your baby's feet, legs, arms and hands, rubbing in the oil and talking to them or singing softly.

6. Use the towel to remove any excess oil when you finish.

Another idea: Try some restful music in the background. Calm, classical music works well (look out for compilations with titles like 'Tranquility', 'Relaxation' or similar).

HELPFUL HINTS
Keep eye contact all the time, and stop if your baby becomes anxious or wriggly.

Take care when picking baby up after massage – oily babies are slippery!

What is your baby learning?

As well as stimulating growth, massaging your baby is important for bonding and leads to confidence and trust.

What is your baby learning?

As well as being soothing, this activity leads to confidence with movement and helps to develop awareness of space.

Swing time
rocking and rolling

What you need:

- *a strong, soft blanket*
- *a soft mat, rug or mattress*
- *a partner or friend to join in*

Ready for more?

Move round in a circle as you swing.

Try 'Row the Boat' and other rocking songs. Say 'Ready, steady, go', with a pause before 'Go', before you start.

DID YOU KNOW?

Stress stops a child from learning. Always ensure your baby is calm and relaxed when you play.

WHAT TO DO:

1. Fold the blanket in half to make a rectangle and lay it on the mat. Place your baby gently on the blanket and gather up two corners each to make a high-sided hammock.

2. Gently lift your baby in the blanket. With a soft and smooth action, swing the baby side to side and sing,

   Swinging, swinging, to and fro,
   This is just the way we go.
   Rocking, rocking, side to side
   Giving baby his (her) first ride.

3. The tune to 'Twinkle Twinkle Little Star' works, but you can always make up your own.

4. Gently lower the blanket back down onto the mat.

5. Watch to see if your baby has enjoyed the activity. Offer, 'again?' Wait for some indication (a glance, a kick, a bounce, or maybe a sound) to tell you that the song and the swing should be repeated.

Another idea: Share the singing, or sing alternate lines. Try moving gently up and down as an alternative to swinging.

Up the arm, down the arm

a singing game

What you need:
• *a blanket, rug or pile of cushions*

Ready for more?

Play the same game 'walking' up and down tummy, back, cheeks. Or gently 'jump' your fingers up and down your baby's arms and legs.

When your baby is old enough encourage him or her to join in the singing.

WHAT TO DO:

1. Lie your baby on the floor on a blanket or rug. If you think they are likely to roll away, put a cushion each side of them.

2. Gently hold one of your baby's hands so their arm is straight. 'Walk' your other fingers up and down baby's arm as you sing or say this song:

   Up your arm, up your arm,
   Walking up your arm.
   Down your arm, down your arm,
   Walking down your arm.

3. As you reach your baby's hand, give a little tickle.

4. Watch to see if your baby has enjoyed the game. Offer 'again?' Wait for some indication, a glance, a kick, or maybe a sound to tell you that the song and walking should be repeated. This time do it on the other arm.

   Another idea: Sit baby up and do the finger walking on their legs.

HELPFUL HINTS

When your baby is old enough, let them do the 'walking' on your arm or hand. They will enjoy the activity and it will develop their muscles as well as strengthening their relationship with you.

Babies and children like routine. Make up some simple songs and games to use at bedtime or change times.

What is your baby learning?

This stimulates the development of memory, and leads to feelings of wellbeing and the growth of trust.

Gently, gently
rock and sing

What you need:
- *No special equipment for this activity.*

Ready for more?

Use ambient music and sound recordings (waves, water, quiet electronic music, etc.) to help provide rhythm and promote relaxation.

When baby is older include a soft toy or teddy to join in the rocking and singing.

WHAT TO DO:

1. Find a quiet spot (a rocking chair, pile of cushions, settee) and sit with your baby supported comfortably in your arms.

2. Look into your baby's eyes and gently rock backwards and forwards

3. Sing a quiet song. You could sing 'Hush a Bye Baby' or 'Row the Boat', or any favourite tune in a quiet voice. Gently stroke your baby's cheek as you sing or hum the tune.

4. If your baby reaches out to touch your face, move closer so you're in range.

Another idea: Play some soft music in the background.

DID YOU KNOW?

Many babies need help to sleep. Being comfortable, warm and calm will help.

What is your baby learning?

This activity helps with focus and eye development, as well as promoting a feeling of wellbeing. It leads to confidence, self assurance and trust.

HELPFUL HINTS

In fine weather do this activity outside, listening to the wind, watching the clouds and the leaves. It doesn't have to be warm, so long as you both wrap up.

Look at your baby a lot, and praise him or her when they look at you. Eye contact is important.

What's around?
exploring near you

What you need:
- *no special equipment, just a good eye for what your home offers*

WHAT TO DO:

1. If your baby is young, carry them to different parts of the room to explore what's there. If your baby is older encourage him or her to crawl.

2. Point to an object, name it, then pick it up and bring it near to them. Give an older crawler the chance to choose.

3. Talk about the object. Use words to say what it looks and feels like – e.g. 'lumpy', 'smooth', 'shiny'.

4. Encourage baby to touch or hold the object by bringing it nearer.

5. Visit a different part of the room (or another room) to look at something else. Choose things that look and feel different from the first ones you picked – smooth/bumpy, shiny/matt, soft and warm/cold and hard.

Another idea: If your baby is able to sit, settle them on the floor and bring objects for them to hold. Sit opposite them to talk about them.

Ready for more?

Collect some objects in a basket. Place the basket in front of baby and let them choose which ones they're going to explore and play with. Some people call such a collection a 'treasure basket'.

Encourage your baby to point to other objects they want to look at. Bring these to them and praise their communication.

What is your
baby learning?

*This activity is good
preparation for imitating
and comparing.*

DID YOU
KNOW?
*Babies have a definite
preference for high
contrast images, such
as geometric shapes
in black, white
and red.*

Go the hole way
exploring holes

DID YOU KNOW?
Some people think that babies are born without kneecaps. Babies do have kneecaps, but they are made of cartilage.

What you need:
- *things with holes – sieves, colanders, plastic tea strainers, plastic tubes*
- *UHT cream in an aerosol can*
- *slotted spoons and spatulas*

WHAT TO DO:

1. Squeeze a small amount of cream into the colanders and explore it with your baby, pushing it through the holes and experiencing the different textures.

2. Pat the cream with the spoons and spatulas, adding more cream as needed to keep the texture interesting.

3. Say or sing a simple commentary, using single words and short phrases, describing how your baby is exploring the cream and holes, such as 'Pat, pat, pat', or 'Push it in the hole' and 'All gone'.

   Another idea: Put some cream on your baby's hands and play 'Round and Round the Garden'.

Ready for more?

If your baby is a little older (6 month+) encourage him/her to isolate their index fingers to make patterns in the cream, or to poke into the holes.

Spread 'hundreds and thousands' sugar strands on a plastic tray and play at sprinkling the tiny strands.

What is your baby learning?

This activity helps develop hand and arm control and encourages exploration, investigation and experiment. It gives opportunities to explore cause and effect.

HELPFUL HINTS

Most young babies won't like cream on their faces and it could get in their eyes, so wipe it off.

Most babies will put the cream in their mouths. Make sure everything is clean, and don't let them eat too much!